Yellow Flower Hat

MATERIALS:
White floppy hat
27" Black & White $\frac{5}{8}$" ribbon
Yellow 5" silk flower
Fabri-Tac Glue

INSTRUCTIONS:
Glue ribbon around hat.
Glue flower to left side of hat.

Rose Hat

MATERIALS:
White floppy hat
3 pieces of 14" long Dark Pink
$2\frac{1}{2}$" wide wire-edge ribbon
3 Green silk leaves
Fabri-Tac Glue

INSTRUCTIONS:
Fold ribbon in half lengthwise.
Turn under end of ribbon.
Roll end to form center.
Loosely wrap ribbon around
center pressing wire to form
gathers. Fold end under, glue.
Glue 3 roses to hat adding 3
silk leaves under roses.

Red Shoes

MATERIALS:
Red shoes
$\frac{3}{8}$" wide ribbon (32" Red,
   32" White, 84" Blue)
2 Blue 1" buttons • E6000 glue

INSTRUCTIONS:
Glue Blue ribbon around
   bottoms of crocs.
Cut Red, White, and remaining
   Blue ribbons into 8" lengths.
For each ribbon glue ends
   together.
Glue 2 Whites, 2 Blues, 2 Reds
   together in center. Make 2 bows.
Glue bows to crocs.
Glue buttons in centers of bows.

Yellow Flip Flops

MATERIALS:
Yellow flip flops
2 Yellow silk flowers
30" Yellow-Orange $\frac{1}{2}$" ribbon
Two 20" Green $\frac{1}{4}$" wide ribbons
Red Liner Tape $\frac{1}{4}$" wide
Fabri-Tac Glue

INSTRUCTIONS:
Stick tape to straps and wrap
   Yellow ribbon around straps
   to cover.
Make 2 Green bows for each
   flip flop and glue to bottom
   of silk flowers.
Glue flowers to flip flops.

Daisy Visor

MATERIALS:
White visor
30" Yellow $\frac{7}{8}$" wide ribbon
Daisies (2 Yellow, 1 White)
3 Green silk leaves
Fabri-Tac Glue

INSTRUCTIONS:
Glue 20" of ribbon around
   visor turning under ends.
Use 10" of ribbon to make a
   bow with one tail.
Cut tail into points.
Glue to right side of visor.
Glue 3 daisies to bow with
   3 silk leaves under daisies.

Pink Flip Flops

MATERIALS:
Pink flip flops
Ribbons (Pink, Black, White)

INSTRUCTIONS:
Cut 24 assorted 6" pieces of
   ribbon for each flip flop.
Tie 12 ribbons on each side of
   center toe piece.
Repeat for second flip flop.
Trim ribbon ends to a point.

Hats and Shoes
Easy to make and fun to wear!

Shirts & Socks

You'll look pretty from head to toe when your shirts and even your socks can make a fashion statement.

White Shirt

It's easy to dress up any shirt by adding sumptuous satin. The satin rose makes this shirt really special.

MATERIALS:
White sleeveless T-shirt
35" wire-edge Dark Pink $2\frac{1}{2}$" wide ribbon
12" Pink satin $2\frac{1}{4}$" wide ribbon
Pink thread and needle • Fabri-Tac Glue

INSTRUCTIONS:
Collar: Pull wire out of one side of ribbon.
Pull both ends of remaining wire to form gathers.
Beginning in center of front, glue ruffle to shirt ending in back.
Glue under ends of ribbon.
Rose: Fold satin ribbon in half lengthwise and sew a long
  Running stitch along edges.
Pull end of threads forming gathers.
Roll end to form center, loosely wrap ribbon around center.
Stitch bottom to hold rose in place.
Glue rose to front of shirt on ruffle.

Black Shirt

Take a simple shirt from stark to smashing in minutes. Black and pink are a sure-fire fashion combination every time.

MATERIALS:
Black T-shirt
Three 14" pieces of Pink $2\frac{1}{4}$" wide satin ribbon
String of pearls • Pink thread and needle

INSTRUCTIONS:
Fold ribbon in half lengthwise and fold both ends under.
Make a long Running stitch close to open edges.
Pull thread to make tight gathers. Knot and trim threads.
Curl ribbon around forming flower. Glue in place.
Tie a knot in a piece of the string of pearls. Glue to center of flower.
Make 2 more flowers and glue to shirt.

Dark Pink Socks

MATERIALS:
1 pair Dark Pink socks
Two 12" pieces of White lace
Two 6" pieces of White-Pink $\frac{1}{4}$" wide ribbon
2 Pink buttons
2 Clear 12 mm rhinestones • Fabri-Tac Glue

INSTRUCTIONS:
Stretch end of sock cuff slightly and glue lace
  to the end.
Make two bows from White ribbon and glue to
  the sock cuffs.
Glue buttons to knots and rhinestones to buttons.

Light Pink Socks

MATERIALS:
Pink socks • Fabri-Tac Glue
Two 5" circles of Pink fabric
2 Clear $\frac{3}{4}$" rhinestones

INSTRUCTIONS:
Yo-yo: Press $\frac{1}{4}$" hem around edge of
  circle. (See page 10 diagrams.)
Sew a long Running stitch on folded
  edge.
Pull ends of thread forming gathers.
Tie ends together.
Glue one yo-yo to each sock cuff and
  glue rhinestones in centers.

White Socks

MATERIALS:
White socks • Fabri-Tac Glue
16" Yellow $\frac{7}{8}$" wide ribbon
4" Orange $\frac{1}{4}$" wide ribbon
2 Clear 8mm rhinestones

INSTRUCTIONS:
Use 8" of Yellow ribbon to make bow
  and tail.
Cut tails into points.
Wrap small piece of Orange ribbon
  around center of bow, glue to back.
Glue rhinestone to center of Orange
  ribbon.
Make second bow, glue bows to socks.

Pink Dress

*Your favorite T-shirt
easily becomes a fancy
dress when you add ruffles
and ribbon.*

MATERIALS:
Pink child size 6-8 T-shirt
$\frac{1}{2}$ yard coordinating Pink fabric
Pink grosgrain 1" wide ribbon to fit
  around bottom edge of shirt
  plus 5" for bow
Pink $\frac{3}{4}$" button
Pink thread
Needle or sewing machine
Straight pins
Fabri-Tac Glue

INSTRUCTIONS:
Cut 1 ruffle 10" x 44" and a second
  ruffle 8" x 44".
Fold 10" fabric in half forming a
  5" ruffle.
Stitch short ends together and press.
Sew a long Running stitch along the cut
  edges (opposite the fold).
Gather and pin ruffle to bottom of shirt
  adjusting gathers.
Stitch in place.
Repeat for 8" piece.
Sew ruffle to shirt 2" above first ruffle.
Glue Pink ribbon to stitching line.
For bow, fold ribbon in a figure 8. Pinch
  the middle and wrap tightly with
  thread. Knot securely. Sew a button
  over the knot. Glue bow to dress.

Dancewear

Every little girl dreams of dancing. Make your daughter's dream come true with these gorgeous outfits.

White Shirt

MATERIALS:
White sleeveless T-shirt
6" wide tulle (2 yards each Lavender, Pink)
26 gauge wire
Wire cutters
Fabri-Tac Glue

INSTRUCTIONS:

For each flower:

Cut 6 pieces of tulle 3" x 6". Place pieces together and accordion fold on 3" side.

Wrap a piece of wire around center several times and twist. Holding wire, separate each layer of tulle forming a puff flower.

Cut wire close to flower and push wire into flower.

Glue flowers to shirt.

Blue and Purple Tutu

SIZE: 22" long

MATERIALS:
Tulle (6 yards Navy, 3 yards Aqua, 3 yards Purple)
3 yards Royal Blue ribbon 1" wide for waistband
5 Blue 5" wide daisies
$\frac{1}{2}$" wide elastic

INSTRUCTIONS:

Skirts:

Cut 4 Navy, 2 Purple and 2 Aqua pieces of tulle, each 22" x 3 yards. Stack all pieces aligning the long edges. Sew the layers together along one long edge with a small Zigzag stitch. The top 2 layers and bottom 2 layers should be Navy.

Waistband:

Sew the top and bottom edges of Royal Blue ribbon onto the tulle $\frac{5}{8}$" from the top edge to create a casing. Measure the waist and add 2" for the length of elastic.

Thread elastic through the casing. Overlap the elastic by 2" and sew the elastic ends together.

Flower Swags:

Gather the top Navy layers into 2 swags in the front and 2 swags in the back. Secure the swags created by the gathers with hand stitches and sew a flower in place. Sew a flower at the center front of the waistband.

How to Make
Waistband Casing

Tutus

Popular since Victorian times, tulle skirts have crossed over from the ballet, costumed events and goth daywear to today's teen party wear. Have fun with these easy-to-make skirts.

Tutus

SIZE: 22" long

BASIC INSTRUCTIONS FOR TUTU SKIRTS:
Cut ribbon long enough to wrap around waist, adding 24" for bow and tail.
Cut 72 pieces of tulle 6" x 44".
Fold each tulle strip in half lengthwise.
Attach each tulle strip to waistband ribbon with a Lark's Head knot.
Trim ends to a point.

MATERIALS FOR WHITE TUTU:
4 White 6" x 25 yard rolls tulle
5 yards 6" wide Pink tulle
56" White 1" wide ribbon for waistband
Needle & thread

INSTRUCTIONS FOR WHITE TUTU:
For each tulle flower: Cut 6 pieces of Pink tulle 3" x 6".
Place pieces together and accordion fold on 3" side. Wrap thread tightly around center several times and knot tightly. Separate each layer of tulle forming a puff flower. Make 10 flowers.
Tie waistband around waist. Decide on the position of the flowers and stitch flowers to skirt.

MATERIALS FOR PINK TUTU:
Four 6" x 25 yard rolls tulle (Light Pink, Medium Pink, Dark Pink)
4 Pink silk flowers
2 yards White satin 1" wide ribbon
Curling ribbon (Light Pink, Dark Pink, Lavender)
Fabri-Tac Glue

INSTRUCTIONS FOR PINK TUTU:
Cut 15 pieces of curling ribbon 45" in length.
Attach ribbon with Lark's Head knot between the tulle.
Glue silk flowers at waist.

MATERIALS FOR BLACK TUTU:
4 Black 6" x 25 yard rolls tulle
2 yards Black satin 1" wide ribbon

INSTRUCTIONS FOR BLACK TUTU:
Follow General Instructions.

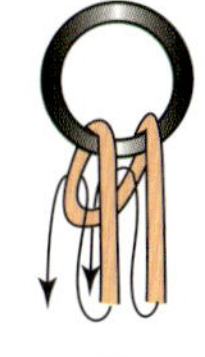

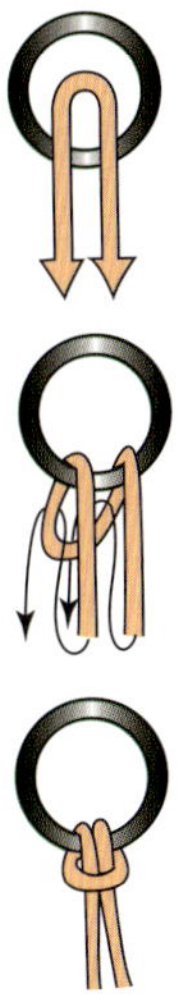

Lark's Head
Knot

Patriotic Visor

Hats off to the red, white, and blue!
Show off your patriotism every day.

MATERIALS:
White visor
21" Red-White-Blue 1" wide ribbon
Star buttons (4 Red, 1 White, 3 Blue) • Fabri-Tac Glue

INSTRUCTIONS:
Glue ribbon around visor, turning under ends.
Glue 3 Red and 2 Blue buttons above ribbon.
Glue Red, White, and Blue buttons to brim.

Patriotic Shirt

MATERIALS:
White T-shirt
Tulip Cool Color Spray (Coral Red, Royal Blue)
Tulip Crystal Glitter dimensional paint
Buttons (16 White $\frac{5}{8}$", 2 Red $\frac{7}{8}$") • White craft thread
Manila folder
Paper towels • Newspaper • Masking tape
Aleene's Tacky Spray adhesive • Fabri-Tac Glue

INSTRUCTIONS:
Cut two 4" squares from manila folder.
Trace a star in the center of each square.
Stick scissors into stars and cut out to make a stencil.
Spray stencil with adhesive and place on shirt.
Stick masking tape around entire design forming an 8" square.
Stick 2 masking tape stripes in empty squares.
Cover all areas of shirt with paper towels except stars.
Spray with Royal Blue. Let dry.
Uncover striped squares.
Cover Blue stars with paper towels.
Spray stripes with Coral Red.
Remove all paper towels and tape. Let dry.
Outline stripes with Crystal Glitter. Let dry.
Glue four White buttons on each White stripe.
Sew and tie White craft thread in Red buttons in stars.

Red Flower Shirt

Summer's flowers sizzle with
passionate color. Share the energy
of the season with this easy shirt.

MATERIALS:
White T-shirt
45" Red $\frac{7}{8}$" wide ribbon
$\frac{5}{8}$" Yellow rhinestone
36" Jumbo Green rick rack
Red thread and needle
Fabri-Tac Glue

INSTRUCTIONS:
Make a Running stitch close to
  one edge of the Red ribbon and
  gather loosely.
Fold under end and wrap ribbon
  around forming flower.
Secure with stitches on the back.
Fold under second end.
Glue flower to shirt.
Glue rhinestone in center.
Cut rick rack into one 11" and
  two 9" pieces.
Glue 11" piece as stem.
Glue 9" pieces as leaves.

Pink Hearts Shirt

Bling makes it beautiful! Here's a fun
way to decorate a shirt. This is a great
project to do with a friend.

MATERIALS:
Pastel Pink T-shirt
Tulip Hot Pink Cool Color Spray
Tulip Crystal Glitter dimensional paint
Rhinestones (2 Clear 12mm, 52 Clear 8mm)
Manila folder
Paper towels • Newspaper • Masking tape
Aleene's Tacky Spray adhesive • Fabri-Tac Glue

INSTRUCTIONS:
Cut two 4" squares from manila folder.
Trace a heart in the center of each square.
Stick scissors into each center and cut out heart,
  making 2 stencils and 2 cut-outs.
Spray stencils and cut-outs with adhesive, position on
  shirt as in photo.
Apply masking tape around entire design forming 8" square.
Cover all exposed areas of shirt with paper towels.
Spray hearts with Hot Pink.
Remove paper towels, stencils, hearts, and masking tape.
Let dry.
Trace 2 hearts with Crystal Glitter. Let dry.
Glue 12mm rhinestones into unpainted hearts.
Glue 8mm rhinestones around painted hearts.

Night Mares

Dressy enough for day-wear, Night Mares can also be worn as a fun night shirt.

MATERIALS:
Oversized adult White T-shirt
2½ yards White eyelet 1" wide lace
Tulip (Petunia Cool Color Spray, Purple Ultra
   Soft fabric paint, Metallic Gold Dimensional
   fabric paint)
Assorted craft threads
11 Clear 8mm rhinestones
Plaid Simply Stamps Jive Alphabet
Star stamp
Manila folder • Paper towels • Paintbrush
Aleene's Tacky Spray adhesive • Fabri-Tac Glue

INSTRUCTIONS:
Trace 2 horses facing each other on manila folder.
Stick scissors into horses to cut out horses
   making a stencil.
Spray back of stencil with adhesive and stick it
   to front of shirt.
Cover all exposed areas of shirt with paper towels.
Spray horses with Petunia. Remove stencil and
   let dry.
Lay shirt on hard surface.
Spell out "NIGHT MARES" with stamps.
Paint stamps with Purple fabric paint and press
   firmly onto shirt above horses.
Paint star stamp with Metallic Gold and stamp
   4 times. Let dry.
Glue 1 rhinestone in each star, above letter I,
   and 3 on each horse's neck.
Cut twelve 6" pieces of craft thread for each horse.
Fold in half and knot. Glue to horses as tails.
Stitch or glue eyelet lace around shirt bottom
   and sleeves.

Best Friends Forever

You'll be decked out from head to toe with a friend.

Tip: Place a sheet of cardboard into garment before spraying or stamping colors.

Coral Shirt

A little decoration adds a lot of pizzazz. Trim out your favorite shirt with this great idea. Add a button to the center of the yo-yo for extra flair.

MATERIALS:
Coral sleeveless T-shirt
36" round shoelaces (2 White, 1 Black)
6" x 6" Black-White print fabric
Needle
White thread

INSTRUCTIONS:
Braid 3 shoelaces together.
Glue the braid to the neck and straps of the shirt. Trim extra in the back and glue the ends together.
Yo-Yo: Cut a 6" circle from fabric.
Press under $\frac{1}{4}$" on the cut edge.
Use a large Running stitch on the folded edge.
Pull ends of thread to form gathers. Tie the ends together.
Glue the yo-yo to the top of the shirt.

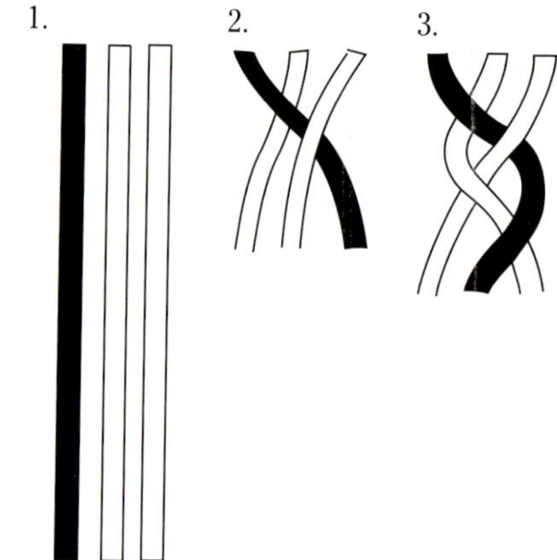

How to Braid Shoelaces

1. Begin with 1 Black and 2 White laces.
2. Follow Step 2 to begin braiding.
3. Your braid will look like #3 when finished.

How to Make a Yo-Yo Flower

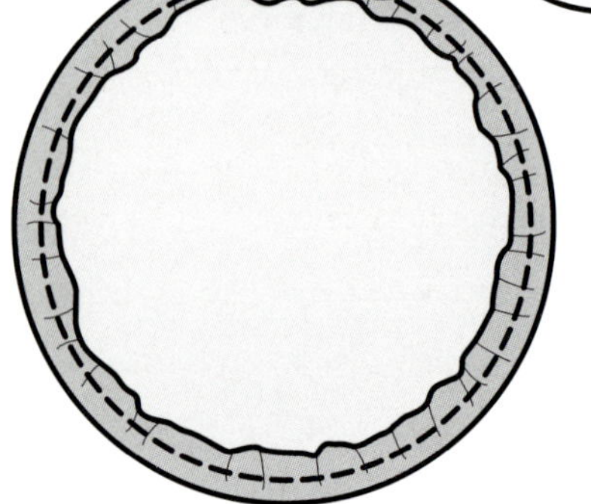

1. Cut a 6" circle from fabric and press under $\frac{1}{4}$" on the edge. With needle and thread, use a large Running stitch on folded edge.

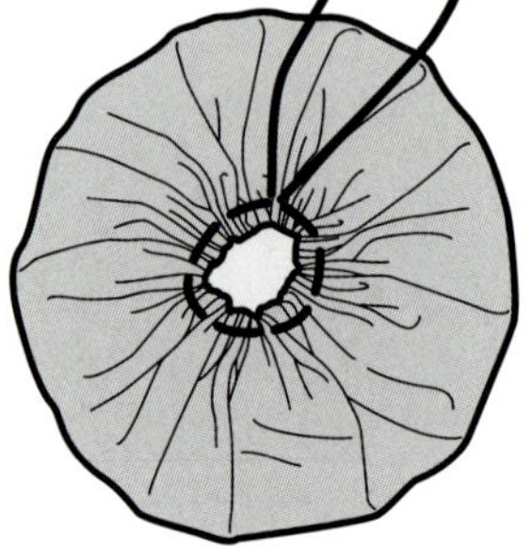

2. Pull the ends of the thread to form gathers. Tuck the fabric edges under then tie ends of thread together.

3. Glue the finished Yo-Yo flower to the top of the shirt.

Show off your love of the game with a sporty matching visor and T-shirt.

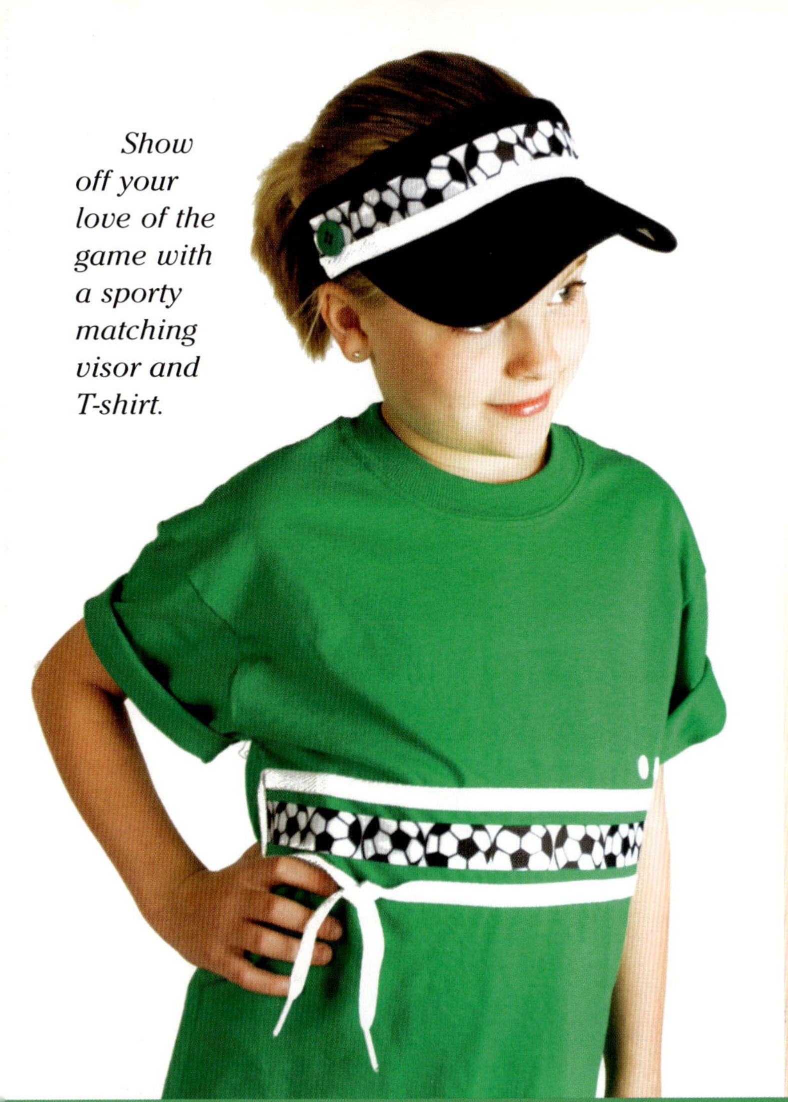

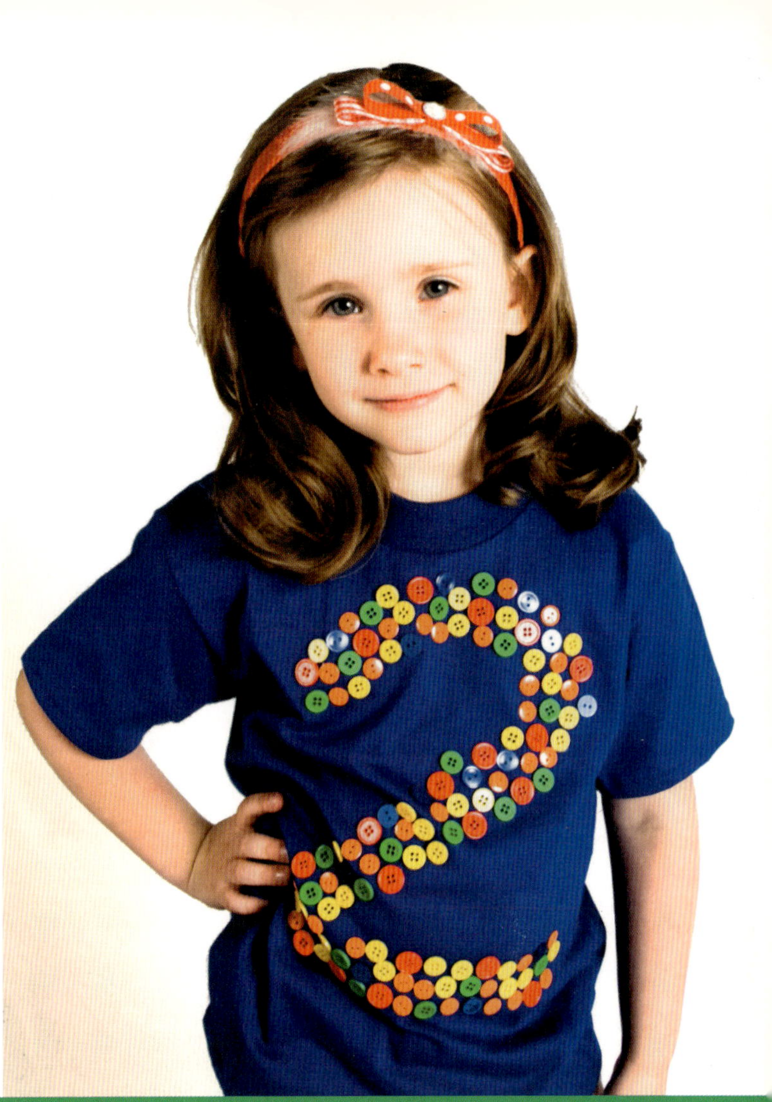

Soccer Shirt

MATERIALS:
Green T-shirt
15" Black-White soccer ribbon 7/8" wide
45" White sports shoelace
3 White 5/8" buttons
Straight pins • Fabri-Tac Glue

INSTRUCTIONS:
Glue soccer ribbon across shirt 1 1/2" from underarm of sleeve.
Pin shoelace in place around ribbon. Leave about 4" hanging.
Tie ends of shoelaces together.
Glue shoelace in place.
Glue buttons above shoelace.

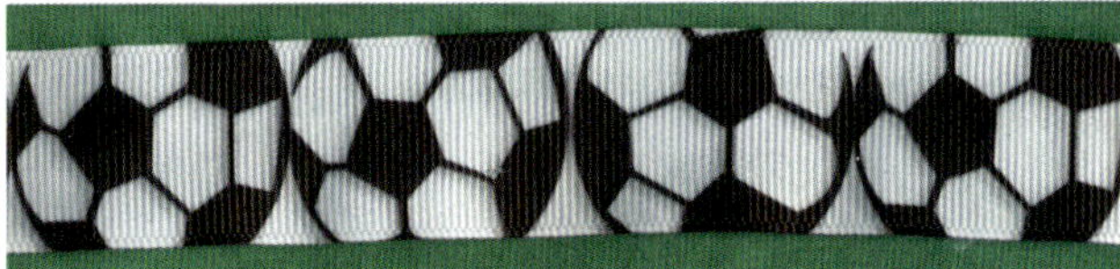

Soccer Visor

MATERIALS:
Black visor
12" White and Black 7/8" soccer ribbon
12" White sports shoelace
2 Green 3/4" buttons • Fabri-Tac Glue

INSTRUCTIONS:
Glue ribbon around the center of the visor. Turn ends under.
Glue the shoelace along the bottom edge of the ribbon.
Glue buttons to the ends of the ribbon.

Cute and Clever Shirts

Nothing brightens your day like a colorful shirt. Decorate your favorite T-shirt in cheerful colors and your favorite design.

Blue Buttons Shirt

Celebrate with a shirt that shows off your colors!

MATERIALS:
Blue T-shirt
125 Bright assorted buttons
Fabri-Tac Glue
Or Buttonhole and Carpet thread and a needle

INSTRUCTIONS:
Empty button package onto shirt.
Arrange into a 2 or any other symbol.
Glue each button to the shirt.
For toddlers, sew all buttons on with a Buttonhole and Carpet thread. Go through each button at least 4 times.

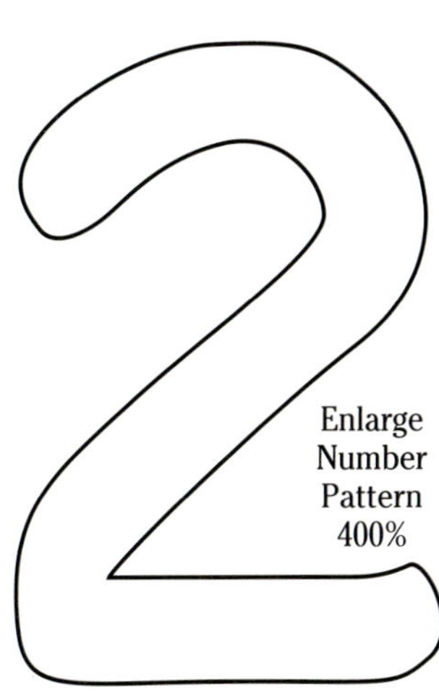

Enlarge Number Pattern 400%

Lime Shirt

Sparkling rhinestones capture the eye when nestled in the center of these pretty fabric yo-yos.

MATERIALS:
Lime T-shirt
6" fabric circles (2 Purple, 2 Light Turquoise, 1 Dark Turquoise)
$\frac{5}{8}$" buttons (2 Lime, 2 Purple, 1 Blue)
5 Clear 7mm rhinestones • Thread and needle • Fabri-Tac Glue

INSTRUCTIONS:
Yo-Yos: Press a $\frac{1}{4}$" hem around the edge of each circle.
Sew a long Running stitch along the hem and gather.
Tie ends together. (See page 10 diagrams.)
Glue yo-yos across top of lime shirt.
Glue a button and rhinestone inside each yo-yo.

Pink Baseball Cap

Create color-coordinated cap embellishments with scraps of fabric and treasures from Grandma's button box.

MATERIALS:
Pink baseball cap
3 fabric squares 5" x 5"
$\frac{3}{4}$" buttons (2 Pink, 1 Blue) • Fabri-Tac Glue

INSTRUCTIONS:
Yo-Yos: Cut three 5" fabric circles.
Press under $\frac{1}{4}$" hem on cut edge.
Sew a long Running stitch along the hem and gather.
Tie ends together. (See page 10 diagrams.)
Glue yo-yos to front of cap. Glue buttons to center of yo-yos.

Blue Shirt

Super simple! Grow a gorgeous garden of flowers on your favorite shirt with no sewing. This inexpensive project is perfect for beginners and groups.

MATERIALS:
Blue T-shirt
Three 8" pieces of Pink $\frac{1}{4}$" or $\frac{3}{8}$" wide ribbon
Three 8" pieces of Purple $\frac{1}{4}$" or $\frac{3}{8}$" wide ribbon
Three 8" pieces of Yellow $\frac{1}{4}$" or $\frac{3}{8}$" wide ribbon
40" Green $\frac{1}{4}$" wide ribbon (25" for stems, 3" for each leaf)
1" buttons (Purple, Orange, Pink)
Yellow craft thread
Fabri-Tac Glue

INSTRUCTIONS:
Glue ends of each 8" piece of ribbon together to form petals.
Glue the 3 Pinks, 3 Purples, and 3 Yellows together in centers.
Cut the Green stem ribbon into 12", 8", and 5" pieces.
Make 4 leaves by gluing the ends together.
Glue 2 leaves to the back of the longest stem and 1 leaf
  to the backs of the others.
Glue the stems with leaves to the right side of the shirt.
Glue 1 flower to the top of each stem.
Tie craft thread in the button holes and knot in back.
Glue buttons to flower centers.

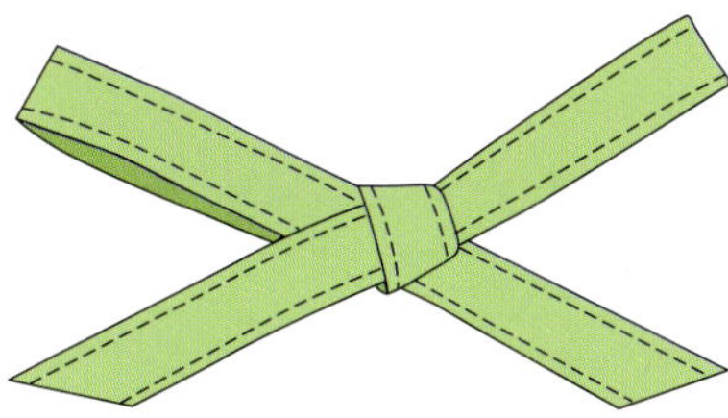

Green Ruffle Shirt

MATERIALS:
White sleeveless T-shirt
44" wire-edge Green striped $1\frac{1}{2}$" wide ribbon
12" Green $\frac{1}{4}$" wide ribbon
Fabri-Tac Glue

INSTRUCTIONS:
Cut the wire-edge ribbon into two 22" pieces.
Pull the wire out of one side of the ribbon.
Gather the wired edge.
Glue the ribbon ends under and glue the ribbon
   across the shirt.
Glue the second ruffle $1\frac{1}{2}$" below the first glue line.
Make a Green bow and glue to the center of the
   top ruffle.

Pink Ribbon Shirt

MATERIALS:
White sleeveless T-shirt
12" Pink striped $1\frac{1}{2}$" wide ribbon
18" Purple $\frac{1}{2}$" wide ribbon
Sewing needle and thread
Fabri-Tac Glue

INSTRUCTIONS:
Glue the ribbon ends under.
Gather the ribbon onto the front of the shirt.
Make a Purple bow and glue to center of the shirt.

Ruffled Pants
by Donna Perrotta

MATERIALS:
White pants
$\frac{3}{4}$ yard fabric
1 yard of $\frac{1}{2}$" wide ribbon
Fabri-Tac Glue

INSTRUCTIONS:
Determine ruffle length:
Measure the cuff and multiply by 2.
Cut fabric:
For bottom tier, cut 2 strips 5" wide by ruffle length.
For middle tier, cut 2 strips 4" wide by length.
For top tier, cut 2 strips 3" wide by length.
Make ruffle:
Fold each piece in half lengthwise and press.
For each pant leg, stack the tiers, aligning the
   raw edges.
Sew the layers together $\frac{1}{8}$" from the raw edges.
Finger pleat the ruffle and sew to the bottom of
   the pant leg.
Tip: If the pants bottom edge will not fit over the
   free arm of your sewing machine, cut the seam
   open for 1" from the bottom.
Glue ribbon over the seam or sew the ribbon in
   place if desired.

Ribbons and Ruffles

*So sweet! Breezy summer outfits are so easy to create
that you'll have them done in a snap. These cute wearables
are perfect for updating the wardrobe on a budget and you'll
have your girls looking pretty in time for the family reunion,
summer camp, or a weekend at the beach.*

Hair Clip Collection

Create a unique accessory to match every outfit in your wardrobe.

MATERIALS:
Metal hair clips 2" - 3" long
5" bloom silk flower • $\frac{1}{2}$" Brown button
Fabri-Tac Glue

Ribbons for Pink/Black bow:
24" Pink 1" wide • 18" striped 1" wide
• 6" Black $\frac{1}{4}$" wide

Ribbons for Green/Pink/Brown bow:
1 yd Brown/Green dot $1\frac{1}{2}$" wide • 1 yd Pink 1" wide
• 27" Brown $\frac{5}{8}$" wide

Ribbons for 2 tiny Blue bows:
36" Blue/White dot 1" wide • 12" White $\frac{1}{4}$" wide

Ribbons for Brown/Green bow:
24" Brown/White dot 1" wide • 24" striped 1" wide
• 6" Brown $\frac{1}{4}$" wide

Ribbons for Lime Green double layer bow:
2 yards Lime Green $1\frac{1}{2}$" wide

Ribbons for Striped/White/Pink bow:
1 yd striped $1\frac{1}{2}$" wide • 30" White 1" wide
• 27" Pink $\frac{5}{8}$" wide • 6" Blue 1" wide

Ribbons for Brown Button bow:
5" Brown 1" wide • 5" Pink check $\frac{7}{8}$" wide
• 5" Pink sheer $\frac{7}{8}$" wide • 5" Brown $\frac{5}{8}$" wide
• 5" Brown/Pink $\frac{3}{8}$" wide
• 5" Brown dot sheer $\frac{7}{16}$" wide • 5" Pink $\frac{1}{4}$" wide

INSTRUCTIONS:

Flower Clip:
Remove bloom from stem. Glue flower to clip.

Basic Instructions for Ribbon Clips:
Form a loop. Pinch and hold the loop. Make a half twist in the ribbon to keep the right side facing you. Form additional loops, pinching between your thumb and forefinger. Using a 6" ribbon, tie the center securely in a knot.

For multi-layered bows, make the base bow first and tie the center but do not attach to the clip yet. Form additional bows with loops slightly smaller than the base. Tie bows together with a coordinating ribbon.

Wrap the tails around the clip. Trim and glue ends to the clip.

Brown Button Bow: Trim ends at an angle or point. Stack ribbons together and pinch in the middle. Tie securely with a Brown ribbon and attach to clip following the Basic Instructions. Glue a button to the center.

How to Make a Barrette Bow

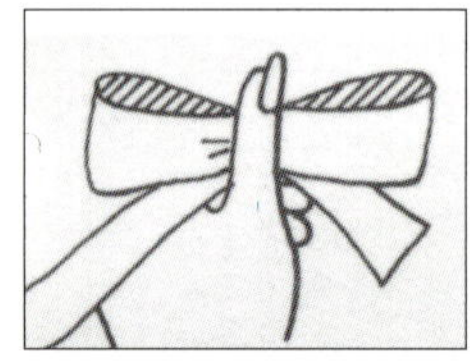

1. With right side of ribbon facing you, grasp the ribbon with thumb and forefinger. Fold the ribbon into 2 loops.

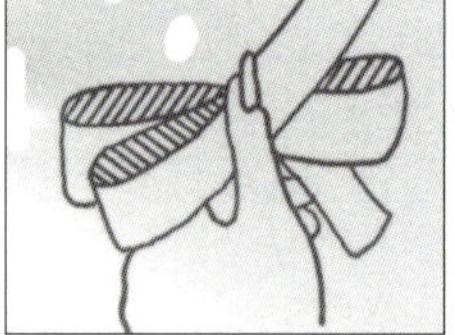

2. Fold the third loop.

3. Fold the fourth loop and tuck the tail under the top fold.

4. Gather the center of the bow and knot securely with a ribbon or thread.

How to Make a Ribbon Bow

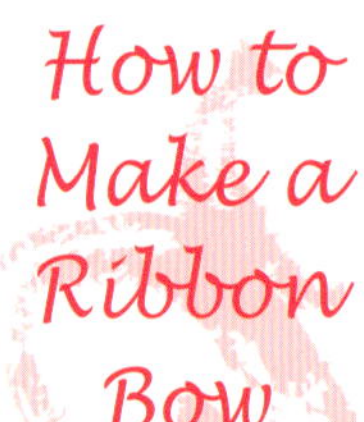

1. Fold ribbon in a figure eight.

2. Pinch in the middle.

3. Wrap the center with another piece of ribbon.

Red Headband

Headbands are in fashion, making them wearable every day.

MATERIALS:
1" plastic headband
25" Red $\frac{3}{4}$" wide ribbon
8" Red-White $\frac{5}{8}$" wide checked ribbon
Red-White $\frac{3}{8}$" wide dotted ribbon (2" and 7")
Clear $\frac{1}{2}$" rhinestone • White feather
Fabri-Tac Glue

INSTRUCTIONS:
Wrap plastic headband with Red ribbon. Glue
  the ribbon and ends as you go.
Make bows from checked and dotted ribbon.
Place dotted onto checked bow and wrap small
  piece of dotted ribbon around bow in the center.
Glue feather to right side of headband and bow
  to feather. Glue a rhinestone to center of bow.

Black Bow Headband

MATERIALS:
$\frac{5}{8}$" plastic headband
30" Black $\frac{3}{4}$" wide ribbon
27" Black-White $1\frac{1}{4}$" wide dotted ribbon
Fabri-Tac Glue

INSTRUCTIONS:
Cut 8" Black $\frac{3}{4}$" ribbon for tying the bow.
Wrap plastic headband with remaining Black
  $\frac{3}{4}$" ribbon, gluing ends.
Make a bow from wide ribbon and glue to
  headband. Tie the 8" ribbon around the bow
  and headband. Secure with glue.

Pink Ribbon Band

MATERIALS:
White stretchy headband
1 yard Pink $2\frac{1}{4}$" wide ribbon • Fabri-Tac Glue

INSTRUCTIONS:
Cut 8" of ribbon for tie. Tie remaining ribbon
  into a bow. Wrap the 8" ribbon around the bow
  center and headband and knot.

Blue Tulle Band

MATERIALS:
White stretchy headband
40" Blue tulle 6" wide • 26 gauge wire
Fabri-Tac Glue

INSTRUCTIONS:
Begin making a fan on the 5" side (accordion
folds). Wrap a piece of wire around center several times. Holding wire, separate each layer of
tulle to form a puff. Cut wire close to flower
and push end into puff. Glue puff to headband.

Pink Flower Band

MATERIALS:
Pink stretchy headband • Pink 3" silk flower
2 pieces of 4" Forest Green $\frac{5}{8}$" wide ribbon
• Fabri-Tac Glue

INSTRUCTIONS:
Glue flower to seam of headband.
Glue ends of ribbon together and glue under
  flower as leaves.

Hair Accents

Next time you need a hair accessory to match your dress, remember these fast and easy ribbon bands.

Fast, fabulous and fun! These quick projects make great favors for a birthday party too.

White Cap

Change a simple cap into something bright in minutes.

MATERIALS:
White stretchy skull cap
5" Pink flower • 2 Green silk leaves
Fabri-Tac Glue

INSTRUCTIONS:
Glue 2 leaves to skull cap.
Glue flower to leaves. Let dry.

Wearables for Baby

by Paula Phillips
Dress your little one in chic attire
without the boutique price tag.

Infant Caps

MATERIALS FOR PINK CAP:
1 Pink infant knit cap
¾" yard of extra large White rickrack
12" of medium Mint Green rickrack
Dritz Fray Check • Thread • Needle

INSTRUCTIONS FOR PINK CAP:
Apply Fray Check to one end of the rickrack and roll into flower shape. Cut 3" pieces of Green rickrack for leaves. Stitch flower and leaves to cap.

MATERIALS FOR BLUE CAP:
1 Baby Blue infant knit cap
6" x 6" Yellow puffy dot fleece • Poly-fil stuffing
Green pom pom • Black floss • #22 Chenille needle
Thread • Sewing machine

INSTRUCTIONS FOR BLUE CAP:
Cut out fish using pattern. Satin stitch the eye with Black floss. With right sides together, sew around the fish leaving an opening for stuffing.
Turn right side out and stuff. Sew the opening closed. Tack fish and pom pom to hat.

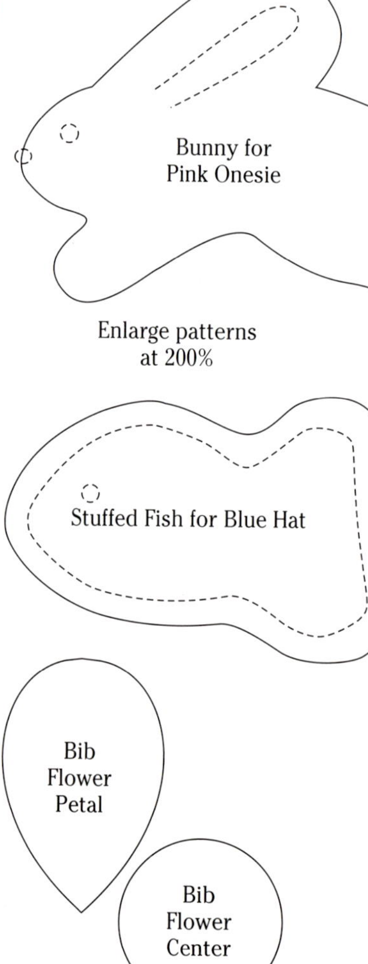

Onesie Jumpers

MATERIALS FOR PINK ONESIE:
1 Pink onesie
5" x 6" White puffy dot fleece
2" x 4" White chenille fabric
5" Pink medium size rickrack
Embroidery floss (Black, Dark Pink)
#22 Chenille needle
Pins • Thread • Sewing machine

PINK ONESIE:
Cut out a White fleece bunny body.
Cut 2 White chenille tail circles.
Pin and sew Pink rickrack to the bunny body to form the insides of the ears.
Embroider the eye with Black floss and the nose with Dark Pink floss.
Applique the bunny to the onesie.
Place tail circles with right sides together and sew around.
Leave a small opening for turning.
Turn right sides out and hand stitch the opening closed.
Hand stitch the tail to the onesie.

BLUE ONESIE:
1 Baby Blue onesie
3" x 5" Yellow puffy dot fleece
5" x 7" White chenille fabric
Black embroidery floss
#22 Chenille needle
Pins • Thread • Sewing machine

BLUE ONESIE:
Cut a Yellow fish body.
Cut 3 fins and tail from White chenille.
Satin stitch the eye to the fish body with Black embroidery floss.
Applique pieces to onesie.

Bibs

MATERIALS FOR FLOWER BIB:
9½" x 9½" bib with Pink trim
Puffy Dot Fleece (⅛ yard Light
Pink, 3" x 3" Yellow)
2 Light Pink bows with pearl hearts
Thread • Pins • Sewing Machine

MATERIALS FOR FROG BIB:
9½" x 9½" bib with Blue trim
7" x 7" Mint Green dot fleece
2" x 4" White chenille fabric
1 Navy Blue gingham bow
Embroidery floss (Light Pink,
  Dark Pink, Black)
Thread • Sewing
machine • Pins
#22 Chenille needle

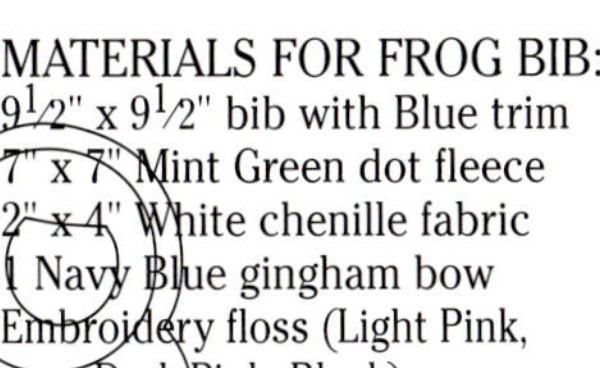

INSTRUCTIONS FOR FLOWER BIB:
Cut 7 Pink fleece petals.
Cut out a Yellow fleece flower center. Pin the flower pieces to the bib.
Machine applique flower to bib. Tack bows near the neck.

INSTRUCTIONS FOR FROG BIB:
Cut out Green fleece body and eyelids.
Cut out White chenille eyes. Machine applique eyes and eyelids to body.
Satin stitch the center of each eye with Black floss and the nose with Light Pink.
Embroider the mouth with Dark Pink floss using a Backstitch.
Machine applique the frog to the bib. Tack the bow onto the neck of the frog.

Enlarge patterns
at 200%

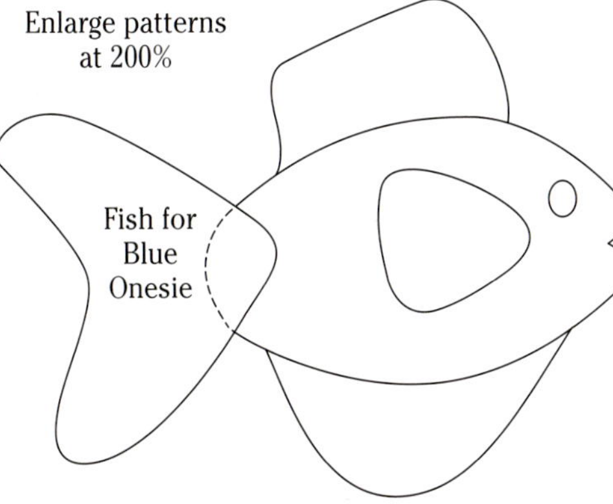

Baseball Caps

MATERIALS FOR BLUE CAP:
1 Baby Blue infant baseball cap
5" x 5" White puffy dot fleece
½ yard Mint Green medium size rickrack
5" Baby Blue medium to large size rickrack
Thread • Sewing Machine • Fabri-Tac Glue

INSTRUCTIONS FOR BLUE CAP:
Cut out a White fleece star.
Sew rickrack pieces in stripes onto the star.
Applique the star onto the front center of the hat.
Glue Green rickrack around the edge of the bill of the cap.

MATERIALS FOR PINK CAP:
1 Pink infant baseball cap
1 Purple silk daisy 4½" bloom
¾ yard multi colored ⅝" wide trim
1½ yards White ¼" wide ribbon
¾ yard sheer Light Green ½" wide ribbon
Wire cutters • Scissors • Fabri-Tac Glue

INSTRUCTIONS FOR PINK CAP:
Starting at the back of the hat, glue trim around the bottom edge.
Remove stem and glue the flower to the right side of the hat.
Cut five 6" pieces of White ribbon and four 6" pieces of the
  Green sheer ribbon.
Fold in half and glue the ends under the flower petals all the
  way around the flower.
With the remaining White ribbon, tie a bow and glue it to the
  center back of the hat.

Kids on Our Block

Create faces that reflect your child with these great 'mix and match' patterns for faces.
Choose hairstyles, eyes, mouths, eyebrows and collars to create an entire neighborhood of friends.

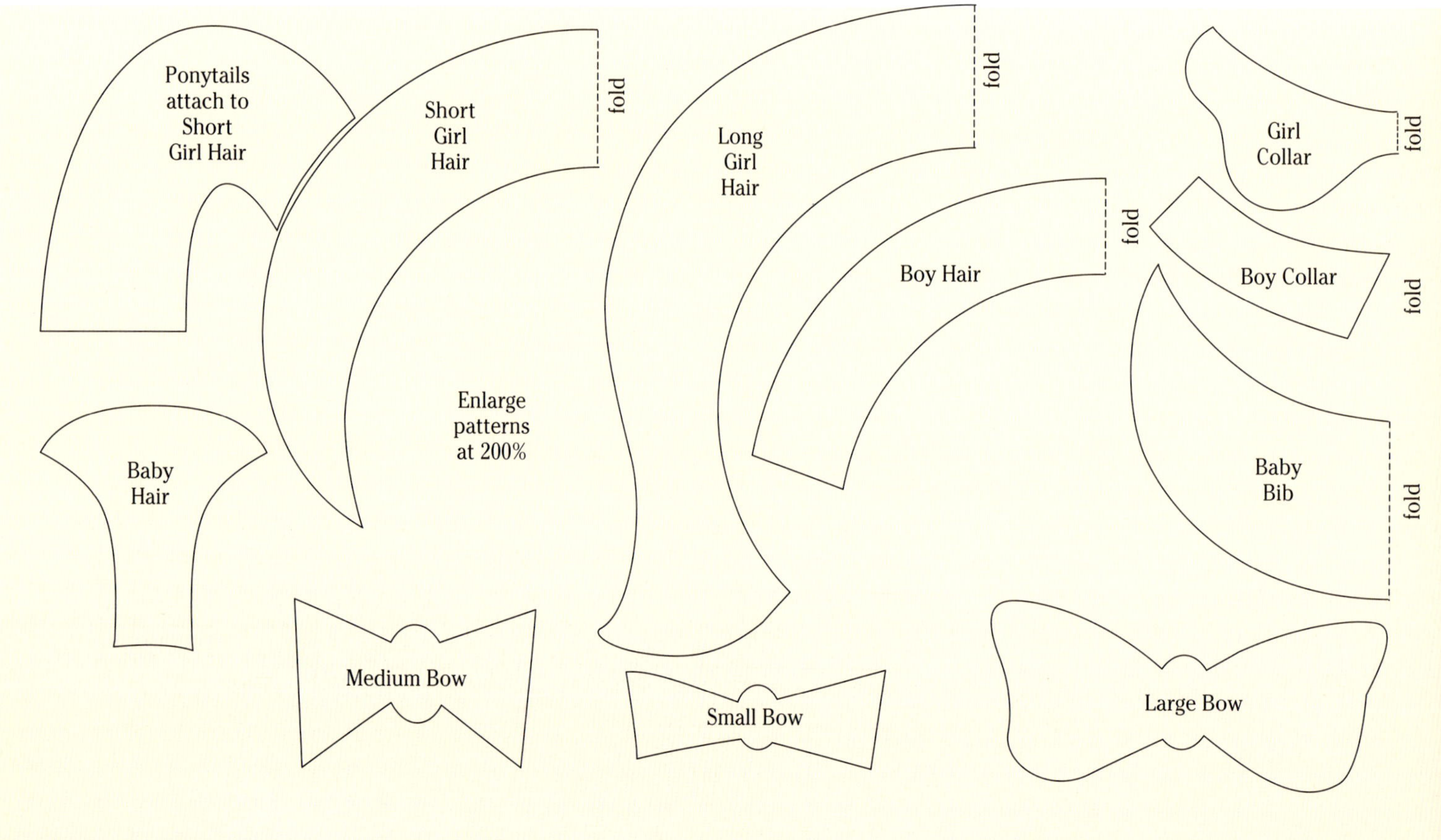

Ponytails attach to Short Girl Hair

Short Girl Hair

fold

Long Girl Hair

fold

Boy Hair

fold

Girl Collar

fold

Boy Collar

fold

Baby Hair

Enlarge patterns at 200%

Baby Bib

fold

Medium Bow

Small Bow

Large Bow

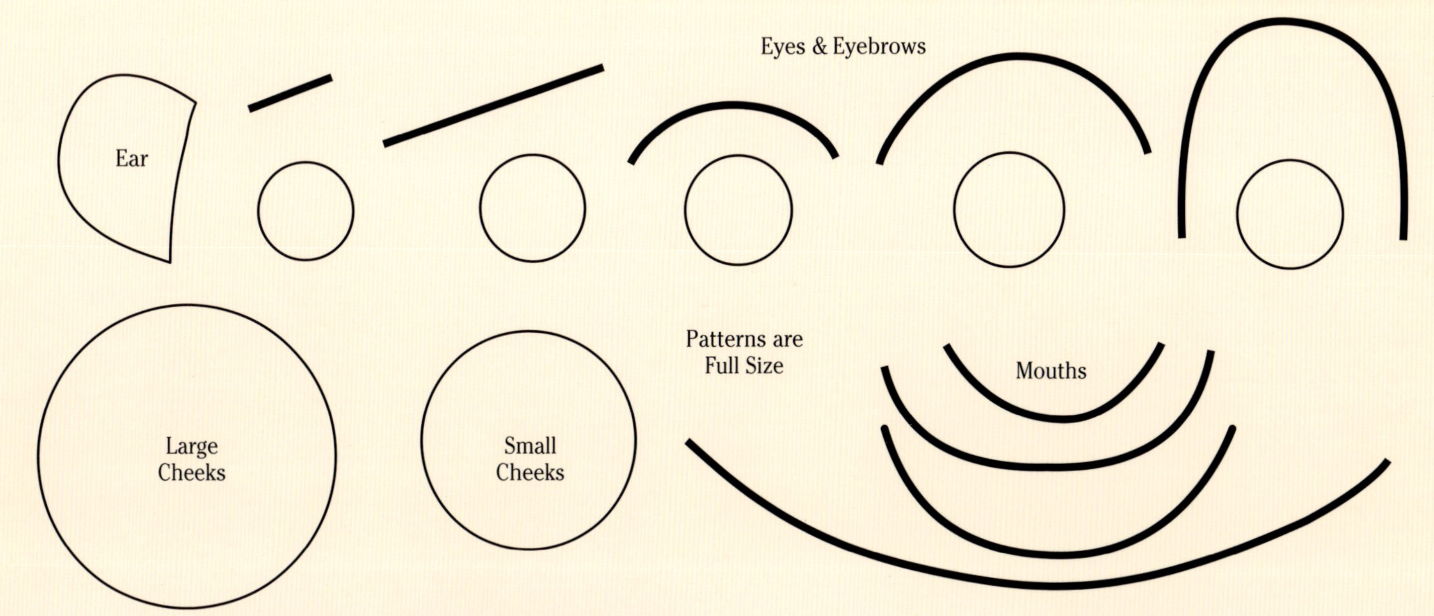

Faces T-shirts
by Donna Perrotta

MATERIALS:
1 colored T-shirt • 8" x 10" washable felt squares
1 yard of iron-on stabilizer • Thread • Needle • Sewing Machine

INSTRUCTIONS:

Shirt Preparation:
Press stabilizer on the inside front of the shirt over the entire area to be appliqued.
Optional Preparation: To create a more easily stitched surface area for small T-shirts, use the following technique. Cut a 4" wide strip of stabilizer and press onto the inside center back of the shirt. Cut the back of the shirt up the center from the bottom to the collar. Do Not cut the collar ribbing. Open the shirt so the inside of the front is easily accessible and press stabilizer over entire area to be appliqued. After appliques are sewn on, sew the shirt back together.

Appliques:
Cut out felt pieces using patterns. Position pieces on front of shirt. Applique using a Zigzag stitch.

Finish: Remove all stabilizer.

Linda Valentino
Linda Valentino has been teaching elementary school in New York for over 30 years. She began designing for magazines 9 years ago and hopes to design full time in the coming years.

Paula Phillips
Paula is an innovative designer who loves all types of crafting and has been published in several craft books. She teaches classes and is a digital designer. You can view more of her work at www.paulaphillips.blogspot.com.

Donna Perrotta
Additional projects and 'Kids on Our Block' T-shirts were made by the talented hands of Donna Perrotta.

Suppliers - Most craft and variety stores carry an excellent assortment of supplies. If you need something special, ask your local store to contact the following companies.

TULIP®FABRIC PAINT & COLOR SPRAY
Duncan Enterprises,
www.ilovetocreate.com
FABRI-TAC® GLUE & KIDS CHOICE GLUE!®
Beacon Adhesives,
www.beaconcreates.com
SIMPLY® STAMPS
Plaid Enterprises,
www.plainonline.com

MANY THANKS to my staff for their cheerful help and wonderful ideas!
Kathy Mason • Kristy Krouse
Patty Williams • Donna Kinsey

Polymer Clay
Dolls & Faces

Design Originals

Can Do Crafts

by Cindy Celusta

Suzanne McNeill

DESIGN ORIGINALS

No. 3354

Making dolls has always been an enjoyable hobby and now it's so easy! You can make faces for a whole gallery of characters with easy to use flexible push molds.

You can also mold hands and feet and add clay pieces to a variety of items from clay pots to boxes to create unique containers for gifts and storage. Or glue the pieces on cards for truly personalized greetings. You will even find instructions for making jumping jack dolls in **Dolls & Faces.**

A few simple supplies, a little time and your creations will come to life!

Suzanne

For a color catalog featuring over 200 terrific 'How-To' books, send $3.00 to

CATALOG
Design Originals
Dept. C-1, 2425 Cullen St, Fort Worth, TX 76107
or visit www.d-originals.com

Polymer Clay
Dolls & Faces

Flexible push molds are a must for everyone who loves to work with clay and make adorable dolls and faces. Simply press clay into a mold then remove it. You can add character lines and other fine details with a needle tool before baking. When baked and cooled, add painted accents to your creations. You'll love the results!

Materials. Sculpey Flexible Push Molds • Sculpey III Clay • Premo Clay • Super-Flex Clay • Liquid Sculpey • Clay Blade • Pasta Machine • Needle Tool • Acrylic Paint • Paintbrush • Doll Hair • Wire • Fabric • Tins • Boxes • Cards

1. Condition clay by warming in hands and form a cone. Press point of cone in nose area and gently push remainder of clay into mold.

2. Trim excess clay from mold with a clay blade. Rub off any clay left on the mold with fingers. Make sure edge of molded piece is clean.

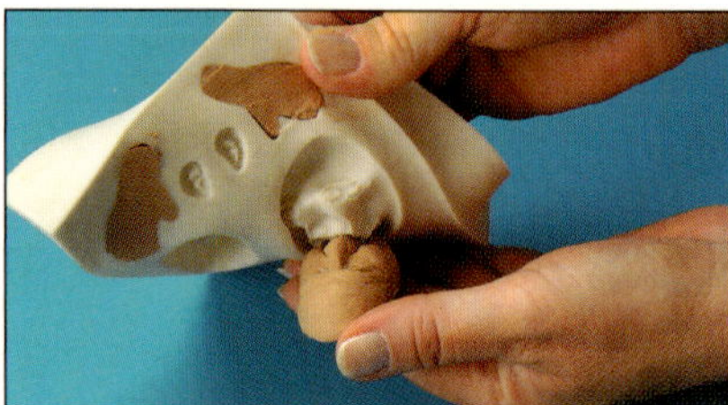

3. For quick release, place mold in freezer for 90 seconds. Press on back of mold, flex and release the clay pieces.

4. Insert toothpick in bottom of head. Roll a small ball of clay and press on back of head. Shape the head and smooth seams.

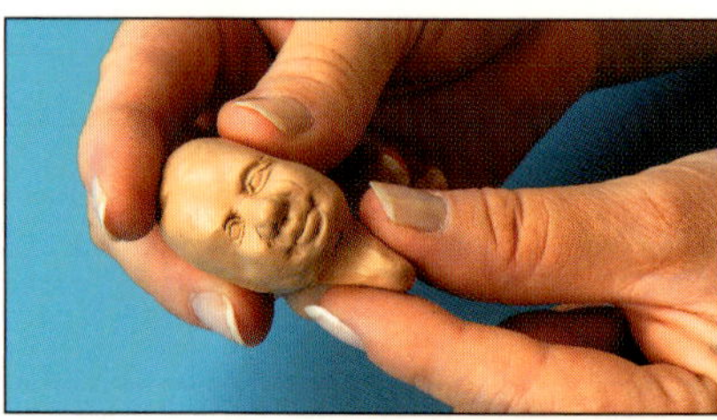
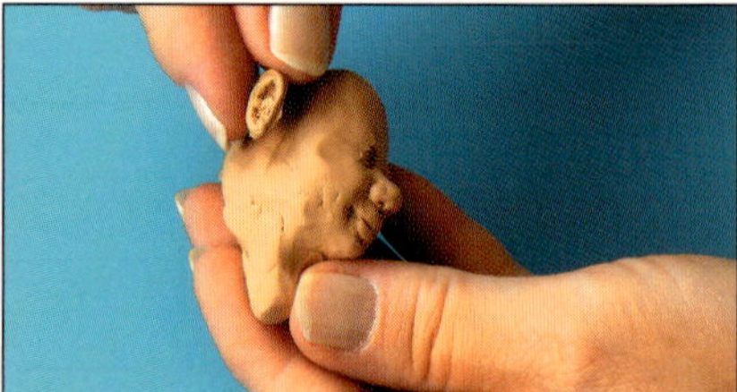

5. Roll log of clay and press on head for neck, smooth seams.

6. Attach the ears to head and smooth edges.

Baking Tips

Gently remove toothpick from neck. Cradle head in a small piece of fiberfill and place on a large baking sheet. Do not allow fiberfill to extend beyond the edges of the baking sheet. Bake the head at 275°F for 30 minutes. Remove from oven and let cool.